Occasional Paper Number Seven

INTELLIGENCE ANALYSIS IN THEATER JOINT INTELLIGENCE CENTERS: AN EXPERIMENT IN APPLYING STRUCTURED METHODS

By MSgt Robert D. Folker, Jr. (USAF)

JOINT MILITARY INTELLIGENCE COLLEGE
WASHINGTON, DC
January 2000

CONTENTS

INTELLIGENCE ANALYSIS IN THEATER JOINT INTELLIGENCE CENTERS: AN EXPERIMENT IN APPLYING STRUCTURED METHODS

Preface

In clear, articulate, unmistakable language, Master Sergeant Folker's learned thesis sets forth the key opposing arguments in the long-standing controversy over the role of structuring in intelligence analysis. The controversy is largely one-sided, because proponents of intuitive analysis see no purpose in debating the issue, as they are completely satisfied with the status quo. It is only the structuring enthusiasts who see a need for drastic change in the way analysis is conducted. Because, as Folker points out, supporters of the status quo include not only most analysts but most commanders as well, the structuring enthusiasts have never made progress in reforming the other side. And they won't make any progress until the superiority of structured analysis over intuitive analysis is proved, which Folker has taken a first giant step in doing.

And it is precisely on this point that Folker challenges the Intelligence Community—indeed the entire U.S. government and the private sector as well—to design and conduct reliable tests to demonstrate which analytic approach is superior: structured or intuitive. Given the wide range of available structuring techniques, each one should be tested in competition with intuition.

There are many myths prevalent in the analytic community, public and private, concerning structured analysis: It is time-consuming and overly complicated; it eliminates the indispensable role of intuition; it involves numbers and arcane formulae that render analysis mechanical and devoid of creative solutions; and so on. Tests like Folker's will surely dispose of these myths and demonstrate the immense value and power of structuring.

His thesis, moreover, should encourage students to undertake research experiments that challenge long-held beliefs and test new theories of military interest. JMIC students are especially well placed to conduct thoughtful, creative research because they bring to this scholarly environment a rich mixture of background and viewpoints, and because they remain vitally involved in the business of wringing meaning from a great variety of intelligence information.

Morgan D. Jones
Former intelligence analyst, supervisor and trainer, Central Intelligence Agency

INTELLIGENCE ANALYSIS IN THEATER JOINT INTELLIGENCE CENTERS: AN EXPERIMENT IN APPLYING STRUCTURED METHODS

Foreword

A growing number of JMIC students have begun to incorporate replicable research design into their theses. This distillation of Master Sergeant Folker's thesis shows how fruitful this approach can be. By taking advantage of on-site research funds available from the College, he managed, in brief visits to four Unifed Command Joint Intelligence Centers, to carry out a controlled experiment to measure the impact of analyst familiarity with and use of one structured analytic technique — hypothesis testing. His findings, if corroborated by follow-on studies, could have a substantial impact on Intelligence Community analytical practices, and even some influence on how senior policy officials react to analytical products. Managers of analytical personnel might also note that structured methods would appear, from this study of non-specialized joint intelligence center analysts, to be useful to specialized analysts who may be required to move beyond their areas of deep expertise to cover new or unfamiliar assignments.

Of equal importance with his findings is MSgt Folker's documentation of applied field research procedures. His subsequent recommendations for follow-on research illustrate the close relationship between doing research and contributing to the corporate learning environment. The Editor welcomes other students to contribute the story of their unique discoveries about the intelligence profession to this series of Occasional Papers.

This paper benefited from reviews by a panel of JMIC faculty, the Director of Research of the Defense Intelligence Agency's Directorate of Intelligence, and by Morgan D. Jones, founder of Analytic Prowess, L.L.C. of Montclair, Virginia.

Russell G. Swenson, Editor and Director, Office of Applied Research,
AFswerg@dia.osis.gov.

INTELLIGENCE ANALYSIS IN THEATER JOINT INTELLIGENCE CENTERS: AN EXPERIMENT IN APPLYING STRUCTURED METHODS

Exploiting structured methodologies compels the intelligence analyst to ana-lyze the intelligence problem at hand and distinguishes analytical endeavors from office administration.

—The author

PREAMBLE

A debate exists between those who prefer to think of intelligence analysis as an art form and those who would highlight the value of a structured, scientific approach to the assessment of intelligence problems. Analytical approaches to intelligence problems can be divided into two overlapping categories—qualitative and quantitative. Qualitative analysis attempts to answer questions or solve problems that are not easily broken down into quantifiable variables. Qualitative analysis is therefore most often used in political, military, and warning intelligence. Quantitative analysis, which uses variables that are more easily measured, generally attempts to solve scientific or technical intelligence problems. Of the two, qualitative intelligence analysis, if performed carefully, arguably provides the information most useful to national policymakers.[1]

A small number of analysts occasionally apply structured methods to qualitative intelligence analysis, but the traditional approach to solve qualitative intelligence problems is non-structured.[2] Surprisingly, no research known to this author has adequately examined whether exploiting structured methodologies will improve qualitative intelligence analysis.

Intelligence analysts who do use non-structured methods for qualitative analysis argue that structured methods too narrowly define a problem and ignore factors that cannot be measured. They assert that their intuitive approach produces superior results. For their part, analysts who employ structured methods for qualitative analysis intuitively believe that structured methods ensure sounder, more comprehensive, and accurate findings.[3] However, no empirical evidence is available to support either belief.

---

[1] Richard K. Betts, "Intelligence for Policymaking," *Washington Quarterly 3*, no. 3 (Summer 1980): 119.

[2] James D. Hammond, *So You Want to Be an Intelligence Analyst?* Research Paper (Washington, DC: Defense Intelligence College, October 1983), 10.

[3] Capt. William S. Brei (USAF), *Getting Intelligence Right: The Power of Logical Procedure*, Occasional Paper Number Two (Washington, DC: JMIC, 1996), 1-2.

The author conducted a controlled experiment among a small sample of non-specialized analysts at four United Command joint intelligence centers to test the effect of applying a structured method to the qualitative analysis of an intelligence problem. Only tentative conclusions can be drawn from the findings in this limited experiment, but the results, if corroborated, have some profound implications for Intelligence Community analysts and their managers.

In brief, the author found that analysts who apply a structured method—hypothesis testing, in this case—to an intelligence problem, outperform those who rely on "analysis-as-art," or the intuitive approach. The modest character of this experiment, and of this finding, clearly calls for follow-on research, but this study at least shows that intelligence value may be added to information by investing some pointed time and effort in analysis, rather than expecting such value to arise as a by-product of "normal" office activity.

THE RESEARCH PROBLEM

Because the Intelligence Community has used technology to increase its ability to collect information, intelligence analysts face an ever-increasing stream of intelligence data.[4] But the Community has not made similar improvements in its analytical capability, and intelligence analysts are not exploiting all of the analytical methodologies available to them.[5] Perhaps in part because intelligence analysts lack familiarity with the proper analytical tools, they are being overwhelmed by the amount of information they are expected to analyze, contributing to "analysis paralysis."[6] Congress is well aware of this phenomenon, and has raised the issue publicly.[7]

A Research Question

A variety of structured methodologies is available to help the intelligence analyst solve qualitative problems,[8] but most analysts display an inability or unwillingness to exploit them.[9] Most people instinctively prefer intuitive, non-structured approaches over structured methodologies. Moreover, identifying all relevant qualitative variables in any

---

[4] Stephen J. Andriole, "Indications, Warning, & Bureaucracies," *Military Intelligence Professional Bulletin* 10, no. 3 (July-September 1984): 8.

[5] David M. Keithly, "Leading Intelligence in the 21st Century: Past as Prologue?" *Defense Intelligence Journal* 7, no. 1 (Spring 1998): 80.

[6] Alvin Tofœr and Heidi Tofœr, *War and Anti-War: Survival at the Dawn of the 21st Century* (New York: Little, Brown and Company, 1993), 158.

[7] Vernon Loeb and Walter Pincus, "New Spy Satellites at Risk Because Funding Is Uncertain, Pentagon Told," *Washington Post*, 12 November 1999, A7.

[8] Robert M. Clark, *Intelligence Analysis: Estimation and Prediction* (Baltimore: American Literary Press, Inc., 1996), 11.

[9] Stephen J. Andriole, senior intelligence researcher and former director of the Cybernetics Technology Office of the Advanced Research Projects Agency, email interview by author, 15 December 1998.

problem is difficult, and quantifying them is daunting. The bottom line: Most analysts prefer a subjective approach.[10] Can intelligence analysts, specifically those conducting analysis in the "softer" sciences such as political intelligence, improve the quality of their analysis by better exploiting structured methodologies? Comparing the analytical results of structured methods with the analytical results derived from traditional non-structured practices used by intelligence analysts should provide valuable insights into improving qualitative intelligence analysis. The need for such an experiment has been clearly identified by a number of specialists.[11]

Improvement in qualitative intelligence analysis has been a goal of long standing in the Intelligence Community, but most attempts to improve the process have ignored analysis and focused on restructuring intelligence organization and providing additional training in non-analytical subjects. The U.S. Commission on the Roles and Capabilities of the United States Intelligence Community determined that too few resources are dedicated to all-source analysis, and even fewer resources are obligated to developing and maintaining analytical expertise.[12] Currently, only six percent of the intelligence budget authorized by the U.S. Congress is spent on analysis.[13] The House of Representative's Permanent Select Committee on Intelligence concluded that "[a]nalytical pitfalls have been recognized in post mortems and other studies of past warning situations, and limited organizational and training efforts have been undertaken in response."[14]

A Record of Analytic Failures

Although organizational restructuring may be of some benefit to the Intelligence Community, the root cause of many critical intelligence failures has been analytical failure. "Failure to predict the North Korean invasion in 1950 was a failure of analysis at higher echelons. ... No analyses accompanied this raw data."[15] The Intelligence

[10] Morgan D. Jones, *The Thinker's Toolkit: 14 Powerful Techniques for Problem Solving* (New York: Random House, Inc., 1998), 8.

[11] Andriole, "Indications, Warning, & Bureaucracies," 12; Stanley A. Feder, "FACTIONS and Policon: New Ways to Analyze Politics," in *Inside CIA's Private World: Declassified Articles from the Agency's Internal Journal 1955-1992*, ed. H. Bradford Westerfield (New Haven: Yale University Press, 1995), 274-275; and Thomas H. Murray, former analyst and trainer for the Central Intelligence Agency and Senior Vice President of Sequoia Associates, Inc., interview by author, 18 January 1999.

[12] U.S. Commission on the Roles and Capabilities of the United States Intelligence Community, "Chapter 8: Improving Intelligence Analysis," in *Preparing for the 21st Century: An Appraisal of U.S. Intelligence* (Washington, DC: GPO, 1 March 1996) URL: *http://www.access.gpo.gov/su_docs/dpos/epubs/int/int012.html*.

[13] Philip Seib, "Intelligence Gathering Remains a Vital Function," 1 March 1999, *Dallas Morning News*, URL: *<http://www.dia.ic.gov/admin/EARLYBIRD/990302/s199990302gathering.htm>*, accessed 2 March 1999.

[14] Andriole, "Indications, Warning, & Bureaucracies," 8.

[15] James P. Finley, "Nobody Likes to be Surprised: Intelligence Failures," *Military Intelligence Bulletin* 20, no. 1 (January-March 1994): 18-19.

Community also failed to predict the Tet Offensive in Vietnam until just hours before the attack. "The analysis failure occurred in where, when, and why."[16] Joseph Nye cites the "analytical disarray in 1978 that prevented the drafting of any estimate about the fall of the Shah, and the 1989 prediction that Saddam Hussein would not make trouble for the next three years."[17] Members of the Senate Select Committee on Intelligence recently voiced their concern about the Intelligence Community's inability to warn of the Indian nuclear tests, calling it the "greatest failure for more than a decade."[18] Others point out that by improving intelligence analysis the Intelligence Community can better support and protect U.S. embassies from terrorist threats.[19]

Some intelligence analysts believe that the ratio of intelligence successes to failures is actually quite good. Arthur S. Hulnick, a notable veteran in the intelligence profession, is one such believer. He stated in a conference paper delivered at the 1987 Annual Meeting of the American Political Science Association that

> the products of the [Intelligence Community] reœect continued growth in the expertise of the analysts, a broader and deeper range of subject materials, and an increasingly sophisticated data base from which to work. Coupled with advances in presentational methodologies, the intelligence product is more useful, timely and relevant than ever before.[20]

Despite his optimism for intelligence analysis, Hulnick agrees that the "analytic process itself is worthy of research."[21]

Because of the Intelligence Community's failures to foresee a number of strategically important foreign developments, intelligence consumers have tended to disregard any analysis of intelligence information. "Whether analysis is good or not, many policymakers will care less about it than they do about collection. They may even resent it, seeing it as naïve speculation by junior bureaucrats that wastes their time."[22] Roger Hilsman, former Assistant Secretary of State for Intelligence Research and Assistant Secretary of State for Far Eastern Affairs, argues that the beneœs of funding a large team of œeld agents is not worth the cost or risk. Covert action tempts presidents into risking the hard work of analysts and diplomats on an "easy œx," damages America's reputation, and is antithetical to a democracy. He concludes that the Intelligence Community should

---

[16] Finley, "Nobody Likes to be Surprised: Intelligence Failures," 20.

[17] Joseph S. Nye Jr., "Peering into the Future," *Foreign Affairs* 73, no. 4 (July/August 1994): 84.

[18] "Don't Blame the CIA," *Economist*, 23 May 1998, 26.

[19] John Kifner, "Raids by U.S. Agents and Tirana Police Reportedly Thwart Attack on Embassy," *New York Times*, 21 August 1998, A13.

[20] Arthur S. Hulnick, "Managing Intelligence Analysis: Strategies for Playing the End Game," *International Journal of Intelligence and Counterintelligence* 2, no. 3 (Fall 1988): 341.

[21] Hulnick, 329.

[22] Richard K. Betts, "Intelligence Warning: Old Problems, New Agendas," *Parameters* 28, no. 1 (Spring 1998): 33.

focus its efforts on improving its analytical support.[23] If the Intelligence Community is to overcome this credibility problem, it must improve its ability to produce accurate, timely, and useful intelligence.

Furthermore, the military's use of precision, information-intensive weapons creates pressure on the intelligence analyst to deliver useful intelligence at faster rates. In the era of modern warfare, fast and precise weapons demand fast and precise intelligence. The intelligence analyst who is unable to conduct analysis quickly can become an information-bottleneck in this environment. It may be arguable that the use of structured analytical techniques helps to speed up the analytical process. This assertion has not been tested, and is beyond the scope of the present research.

Terms of Reference

Quantitative intelligence analysis separates the relevant variables of a problem for credible numerical measurement. Qualitative intelligence analysis breaks down topics and ideas that are difficult to quantify into smaller components for better understanding.[24] Structured methodologies are various techniques used singly or in combination to separate and logically organize the constituent elements of a problem to enhance analysis and decisionmaking.[25] Some structured methodologies, such as organized brainstorming techniques, complement the analyst's intuition and facilitate creativity.

Non-structured methodology is intuitive. Intuition is a feeling or instinct that does not use demonstrative reasoning processes and cannot be adequately explained by the analyst with the available evidence. For the purposes of this study the term "improve," when referring to qualitative intelligence analysis, means to increase, either singularly or in any combination, without decreasing, either singularly or in any combination, the accuracy, specificity, or timeliness of the result.

This study assumes that exploiting structured methodologies for qualitative intelligence analysis does not invariably subordinate one's intuition, education, or experience. The analyst must still make a conscious choice as to whether he will accept a conclusion based on exploiting a structured method or reject it in favor of his intuitive judgment. Moreover, intuition plays an inescapable role in analysis. However, although intuition can usually be relied upon to provide effective solutions to simple problems, it cannot cope with the highly complex problems that routinely face intelligence analysts.

Many factors affect the quality of intelligence analysis. This study is limited to arguing how structured methodologies may influence the results of qualitative intelligence analysis. Due to time and cost considerations, it was necessary to restrict the scope of the

---

[23] Roger Hilsman, "Does the CIA Still Have a Role?" *Foreign Affairs* 74, no. 5 (September/October 1995): 104-116.

[24] Clark, 30.

[25] Jones, xi-xvi.

experiments to intelligence analysts at four of the nine Joint Intelligence Centers (JICs) of the United Commands. Specifically, experiments were conducted with intelligence analysts from the U.S. Special Operations Command (SOCOM), the U.S. Central Command (CENTCOM), the U.S. Southern Command (SOUTHCOM), and the U.S. Joint Forces Command (JFCOM), formerly Atlantic Command (ACOM). Because of these limitations, the evidence presented here should be considered only provisional, not conclusive.

THE ART OR SCIENCE DEBATE

A long-standing debate exists within the Intelligence Community about whether more should be invested in structured methodologies to improve qualitative intelligence analysis. At the heart of this controversy is the question of whether intelligence analysis should be accepted as an art (depending largely on subjective, intuitive judgment) or a science (depending largely on structured, systematic analytic methods). Resolving this question is necessary to provide direction and determine an efficient and effective approach to improve analysis. If qualitative intelligence analysis is an art, then efforts to improve it should focus on measuring the accuracy of one's intuition, selecting those analysts with the best track record, and educating them to become experts in a given field. If, on the other hand, qualitative intelligence analysis is a science, then analysts should be trained to select the appropriate method for a given problem from a variety of scientific methodologies and exploit it to guide them through the analytical process.

Qualitative Analysis as an Art

Proponents of this argument contend that qualitative intelligence analysis deals with an infinite number of variables that are impossible to operationalize because they cannot be adequately quantified or fully collected. A foreign nation that attempts to conceal or disguise information on many of the same variables that an analyst seeks will further complicate the analytical function. Because in many cases the variables are so complex, countless, and incomplete, attempting to analyze them using scientific methods is pseudo-science.[26] Therefore, any attempt to make predictions based on quantifying these variables is futile.[27]

Other arguments attack the rational-actor assumption made by most scientific approaches to qualitative intelligence analysis. "Science can be of little help when dealing with the often irrational and unpredictable human mind."[28] But these critics acknowledge that the traditional approach to qualitative analysis, being an art, is vulnerable to failure — "humans are still fallible in matters of analysis and response."[29]

---

[26] Richard K. Betts, "Surprise, Scholasticism, and Strategy: A Review of Ariel Levite's *Intelligence and Strategic Surprises* (New York: Columbia University Press, 1987)," *International Studies Quarterly* 33, no. 3 (September 1989): 338.

[27] John L. Peterson, "Forecasting: It's Not Possible," *Defense Intelligence Journal* 3, no. 2 (Fall 1994): 37-38.

[28] Finley, "Nobody Likes to be Surprised," 40.

Those who advocate that qualitative intelligence analysis is an art maintain that the most successful analysts take an inductive approach, "in which powers of pattern recognition are enhanced and intuition is elevated."[30] They insist that this approach will lead to more creative and original analysis. They argue that qualitative intelligence analysis is an art because it is an intuitive process based on instinct, education, and experience.[31] Gary Klein, a cognitive psychologist and pioneer in pattern recognition, makes some convincing arguments to support this claim. He challenges the practicality of using scientific methods for qualitative intelligence analysis outside the classroom.

"It is time to admit that the theories and ideals of decisionmaking we have held over the past 25 years are inadequate and misleading, having produced unused decision aids, ineffective decision training programs and inappropriate doctrine."[32] He continues:

> The culprit is an ideal of analytical decisionmaking which asserts that we must always generate options systematically, identify criteria for evaluating these options, assign weights to the evaluation criteria, rate each option on each criterion and tabulate the scores to find the best option.... The technical term is multiattribute utility analysis.[33]

He concludes that:

> [t]hese strategies sound good, but in practice they are often disappointing. They do not work under time pressure because they take too long. Even when there is enough time, they require much work and lack flexibility for handling rapidly changing field conditions.[34]

It is important to note that the majority of Klein's research has been conducted with leaders in the armed forces and emergency service providers such as firemen, but not specifically members of the Intelligence Community. There has always been a clash of cultures between operators (commanders and other decisionmakers whose focus is on accomplishing the mission at hand) and intelligence analysts. As intelligence analysts have attempted to bridge the gap between the two cultures, they have tended to adopt the same intuitive decisionmaking strategies commonly used by operators.[35]

---

[29] James P. Finley, "Intelligence Failure Matrix," *Military Intelligence Professional Bulletin* 20, no. 1 (January-March 1994): 14.

[30] Tom Czerwinski, ed. *Coping with the Bounds: Speculations in Nonlinearity in Military Affairs* (Washington: National Defense University, 1998), 139.

[31] Czerwinski, 139.

[32] Czerwinski, 140.

[33] Czerwinski, 140.

[34] Czerwinski, 141.

[35] The relationship between operators and intelligence analysts has also been the subject of much controversy. For a good summary see Jack Davis' article "The Kent-Kendall Debate of 1949," *Studies in Intelligence* 35, no. 2 (Summer 1991): 37-49.

Science May Offer Only Minimal Analytic Improvements. One argument against the value of structured analysis is that intelligence failures may less accurately be attributed to problems with analysis than to "the decisionmakers who consume the products of intelligence services."[36] Given that intelligence consumers can and do perform their own analysis of intelligence information, they may care less about others' analysis than about collection issues, for example.[37] Nonetheless, if analysts were to make it possible for policymakers to focus "on the methodologies of competing intelligence producers, they would be more sensitive to the biases and leaps of faith in the analyses passed to them,"[38] even if the improvement in quality of analysis were minimal. Opponents of scientific methodologies further claim that, because qualitative intelligence analysis is largely an intuitive exercise, analysts should be encouraged to specialize and be educated into becoming experts in their field. These opponents question the validity of scientific methods and object to others who would use such methods to challenge their expert opinion. To improve analysis, they argue, the analyst must improve his intuitive ability by gaining "area knowledge" through frequent contact with the subject of his study. In the face of these challenges, however, and prior to further debating to what degree the quality of analysis may be improved by using structured methods, the basic research question remains unanswered: Will the use of structured methods improve qualitative intelligence analysis?

A Rebuttal. At first glance it seems that opponents of the scientific approach are criticizing the results of scientific methods. Yet they offer no empirical data to show which approach produces more accurate results, the scientific or the intuitive. The critics do denounce the amount of time it takes to scientifically analyze a problem. However, one should recognize that there are many scientific methodologies available to aid decisionmaking, and selecting and using one need only be as complicated and time-consuming as the analyst wishes.[39]

Unquestionably, the complexity of some scientific methodologies prevents them from being regularly exploited by most intelligence analysts. A graduate of the Joint Military Intelligence College (JMIC) made the following observation in his Masters thesis:

> A major issue common to all the methods is customer acceptance. Due to the highly mathematical nature of [Bayesian Decision Analysis], many users will feel uneasy trusting the resulting assessments. This will only be overcome through proper training of the analysts using [Bayesian Analysis] and repeated exposure to Bayes on the part of decisionmakers.[40]

---

[36] Richard K. Betts, "Analysis, War, and Decision: Why Intelligence Failures Are Inevitable," *World Politics* 31, no. 1 (October 1978): 61.

[37] Betts, "Intelligence Warning: Old Problems, New Agendas," 26-35.

[38] Betts, "Analysis, War, and Decision: Why Intelligence Failures Are Inevitable," 83.

[39] Lieutenant Colonel W. Frank Ball, USMC (Ret.), and Morgan D. Jones, "Improving Marine Commanders' Intuitive Decisionmaking Skills," *Marine Corps Gazette* (January 1996): 63-64.

[40] Captain David Lawrence Graves, USAF, *Bayesian Analysis Methods for Threat Prediction*, MSSI Thesis (Washington: Defense Intelligence College, July 1993), second page of Abstract.

Nevertheless, this lack of confidence should not be allowed to stand as a sweeping indictment of other, more simple and appropriate methodologies.

It is apparent that what these critics are saying is that no one in the heat of producing actionable intelligence uses the scientific approach, so why bother? This brings up two important questions:

(1) Which analysts, if any, are exploiting scientific methodologies when conducting qualitative intelligence analysis?

(2) Which approach (the intuitive or the scientific) produces the more accurate, timely, and useful result?

Other critics concede that utilizing scientific approaches to solve qualitative intelligence problems may improve the product of analysis, but they argue that the benefits are only minor. They insist that allocating resources to other areas such as reorganizing the intelligence bureaucracy, increasing manpower, and improving communication will better improve the intelligence product. One cannot deny that a host of factors affects the quality of intelligence analysis, but improvements to the process do not have to be pursued through a linear approach, nor should effort be wasted trying to determine which approach will yield the most significant improvement. If there is sufficient evidence that a reform promises improvement, it should be pursued.

Qualitative Intelligence Analysis as a Science

A few analysts see qualitative intelligence analysis as a science. Since 1973 the Central Intelligence Agency (CIA) has experimented with quantitative methods in an attempt to apply innovations in the behavioral sciences to political intelligence analysis.[41] At that time neither the Departments of State nor Defense had attempted to integrate quantitative methodologies into their political intelligence production.[42] Much of the effort to incorporate quantitative methodologies into the realm of qualitative intelligence analysis was rejected by analysts because the scientific methods were thought to be too narrowly focused and not relevant to the questions the intelligence analysts were addressing. Most analysts tended "to be skeptical of any form of simplification inherent in the application of probabilistic models."[43]

In spite of the skepticism, advocates of using a more scientific approach in qualitative intelligence analysis assert that science is a necessary tool to use when conducting qualitative analysis. They argue that, although it is impossible to consider every variable when conducting analysis, one can identify key variables and weigh their importance. And although much may be unknown, identifying what is known and analyzing it

---

[41] Richards J. Heuer, Jr., "Adapting Academic Methods and Models to Government Needs," in *Quantitative Approaches to Political Intelligence:* The CIA Experience, ed. Richards J. Heuer, Jr. (Boulder: Westview Press, Inc., 1978), 1.

[42] Heuer, 2.

[43] Heuer, 6.

scientifically is an effective approach. As one Intelligence Community advocate of a more scientific approach to intelligence analysis notes, the identification and use of big-picture, strategic insights can yield intelligence of more value than merely continuing to try to fathom, through the "art of intelligence," transient ideographic actors or their actions: "[Y]ou can disregard [military or political leaders'] madness and genius more readily than societal, economic, or political trends (which are scientifically identifiable) in analysis."[44]

Proponents of qualitative analysis as a science argue that scientific methods help analysts determine the relevancy of information and form conclusions, a process that analysts do not perform well on their own. Hall makes the point that:

> in the absence of concrete guidance or structure[,] analysts generally don't do well in forming conclusions and in discerning relevancy.... They sometimes have difficulty in figuring out relationships among seemingly unconnected pieces of information and in forming fragments of information into a coherent whole.[45]

If qualitative intelligence analysis is art, there is also a concern that the artist will fall in love with his art and be reluctant to change it even in the face of new evidence. The more scientific and objective approach encourages the analyst to be an honest broker and not an advocate.

Science in Other Types of Qualitative Analysis. Scientific methods have been used effectively to assist qualitative analysis in areas outside intelligence. An article in *The Economist* discusses the use of mathematical formulas to solve "normal" business problems that most managers argued could not be solved through quantitative approaches.[46] These managers argued that in their decisionmaking process they practice an intuitive art rather than a rational science. However, science and the use of quantitative methodologies in this case proved to be a more systematic and profitable approach than instinctive trial-and-error. Although many of the managers remained skeptical that such methods would continue to work, these methods do provide another approach to decisionmaking that should not be ruled out without evidence from comparative testing.

Although still not a standard practice in the private sector, some companies are increasingly exploiting quantitative methods and technology to help them make better decisions, increase profits, and compete in the information revolution.[47] If applying quantitative methodologies to qualitative analysis facilitates management of technological

---

[44] Captain David T. Resch, USA, "Predictive Analysis: The Gap Between Academia and Practitioners," *Military Intelligence Professional Bulletin* 21, no. 2 (April-June 1995): 27.

[45] Lieutenant Colonel Wayne M. Hall, USA, "Intelligence Analysis in the 21st Century," *Military Intelligence Professional Bulletin* 18, no. 1 (January-March 1992): 9.

[46] "Art Hammer: The Numbers Man," *Economist*, 8 August 1998, 56.

[47] Rod Newing, "Consumer Information is the Fuel of a New Industrial Revolution," *Financial Times*, 3 February 1999, B7.

information, it stands to reason that the Intelligence Community can selectively use this same approach to improve qualitative intelligence analysis.

Inside and Outside of the Classroom. Many proponents of exploiting scientific methodologies to aid intelligence analysis assume that these methods are regularly used in real-world analysis. Hulnick presents the typical view:

> Advances in analytic methodology seem to have grown remarkably in the past decade. While a discussion of explicit methods goes beyond the scope of this article — and the knowledge of the author — a wide variety of ways of attacking a problem exists. Managers of intelligence must assume that analysts try different techniques, sometimes by giving the problem to separate groups for analysis by different disciplines, sometimes by seeking an outside expert to provide competing analysis.[48]

The former chief of the Analytic Support Group in the CIA's Directorate of Intelligence agrees with Hulnick. "An analyst must have a repertoire of analytic techniques to apply in problem solving. There now exists a rich set of analytic techniques such as pattern analysis, trend prediction, literature assessment, and statistical analysis."[49] The president of Evidence-Based Research, Inc., also expressed the opinion that most intelligence analysts use some type of systematic approach when conducting qualitative intelligence analysis.[50]

This assumption that intelligence analysts use these various scientific approaches is based not on empirical evidence, but on the belief that experience alone does not make an expert, and that an expert must have a tool for structuring knowledge to efficiently solve a problem. Yet the numerous interviews conducted in support of this study, among intelligence analysts from all different agencies and backgrounds, positively invalidate this assumption. Of the 40 intelligence analysts interviewed in direct support of this study, only one maintained that he regularly used a structured methodology (link analysis) and could adequately explain the method and provide current examples of his work.[51] Although the other analysts who attempted to explain their analytical methodology described how they were tasked and how they collected information and prepared it for dissemination, they consistently and strikingly made no mention of analysis. The interviews serve only to confirm Klein's more detailed study: "After studying over 150 experienced decisionmakers and 450 decisions, we concluded that [the intuitive] approach to decisionmaking is typical."[52]

---

[48] Hulnick, 331-332.

[49] Clark, 11.

[50] Richard E. Hayes, president of Evidence-Based Research, Inc., interview by author, 9 February 1999.

[51] Tim DiPace, U.S. Atlantic Command Anti-Terrorism/Force Protection Officer, interview by author, 19 March 1999.

[52] Czerwinski, 144.

In further support of the author's findings, JMIC graduate Stewart Eales notes:
Evaluating the analytical effort in the PURPLE SUNSET wargame is difficult
because there was so little to measure. Despite assertions by some that 'the analyst is at the center of the intelligence process,' the... students virtually ignored
analysis. ... As a result, there was little time or effort dedicated to thoughtful
analysis and dissemination.[53]

This observation was confirmed during the interviews with the JIC analysts. A
repeated complaint was the analyst's lack of time to devote to thoughtful intelligence
analysis. In a separate interview at CIA, it was revealed that in spite of most intelligence
analysts having a broad definition of what analysis involves, they spend little time or
effort conducting analysis.[54]

As noted earlier, Betts asserts that many policymakers see little or no value in
intelligence analysis because it is based on the views of less experienced personnel.[55] This
may be the case because so many intelligence analysts are reluctant to exploit scientific
methodologies, and most intelligence analysts are junior to the decisionmakers they
support. Decisionmakers typically form conclusions based on intuition developed through
years of experience. Therefore, the intelligence analyst who provides an assessment based
on inexperience and his own (lesser developed) intuition should not expect to be taken
seriously. To be credible the analyst must use objective scientific methodologies to
support his conclusions.

While the research for this study sought to collect definitive evidence of frequent and
widespread use of scientific methodologies within the Intelligence Community, only rare
anecdotal information could be obtained showing that such methodologies are actually
used by intelligence analysts in real-world situations, despite the ready availability of
these methods. The National Warning Staff, for example, uses only one quantitative
analytical methodology, a modified-Bayesian technique.[56]

A lack of expertise in exploiting scientific methodologies appears to be at the root of
the Intelligence Community's failure to use them. One cannot expect intelligence analysts
to exploit these methodologies unless they are trained how to select the appropriate
analytical method and apply it to a real-world analytical problem. Analysts at the CIA
have made use of computer programs, such as FACTIONS and Policon, based on a
quantitative methodology, to assist in political analysis and warning. In one application,
while both intuitive-based and scientific-based political intelligence forecasts were
accurate about 90 percent of the time, intelligence analysts using Policon provided more
specific and less ambiguous intelligence.[57] Although this example provides limited

[53] Stewart C. Eales, *Playing with Intelligence: Officer Application of Intelligence in the PURPLE
SUNSET Wargame*, MSSI Thesis (Washington, DC: JMIC, August 1997), 121-122.

[54] An analytic methodologist in CIA's Directorate of Intelligence, interview by author, 29 April
1999.

[55] Betts, "Intelligence Warning: Old Problems, New Agendas," 33.

[56] Warning analyst at the National Warning Staff, interview by author, 05 November 1998.

[57] Feder, 274-275.

documentation, it raises the question, why do not other members of the Intelligence Community share, compare, and exploit these methodologies?

Qualitative Intelligence Analysis as Both Art and Science

The fallacy in the art or science debate may be the "either/or" proposition. If qualitative intelligence analysis is not exclusively an art nor a science, then it may best be considered a combination of both intuitive and scientific methods:

> In our world is an infinite set of problems which have no logically consistent answer; there are some problems which any framework alone cannot solve. ... Yet strategists must not live by inspiration alone. Inspiration unsupported by rigorous analysis becomes adventurism [sic]. Thus intuitive gifts must be paired with an effective theoretical framework.[58]

Availability of Structured Methodologies

In order to expand the applicability of quantitative methodologies to qualitative problem solving, relatively uncomplicated methods have been developed to help intelligence analysts structure their analysis. These structured methods, which can be applied to a broad range of problems and do not focus exclusively on mathematical solutions, provide a scientific and demonstrable approach to analysis that can enhance the intelligence analyst's objectivity. Structured methodologies do not try to replace the subjective insight of the intelligence analyst. Instead the intent is to use a logical framework to illustrate and capitalize on intuition, experience, and subjective judgment.

Some publications do identify which methods are best suited to solve particular types of analytical problems,[59] but not all intelligence analysts receive training in these methodologies. Morgan Jones, a former analyst for the CIA, has recently added *The Thinker's Toolkit: 14 Powerful Techniques for Problem Solving.* This book presents 14 structured methods to aid analysis and decisionmaking. Although it is written for both business and personal use, the structured methods he discusses are among those taught to the fraction of Intelligence Community analysts who enroll at the Joint Military Intelligence College or other intelligence schools.

Numerous other books and software are dedicated to teaching an analyst how to apply one specific structured methodology. The Rand Corporation, for example, offers a book providing a specific methodology for predicting ethnic conflict. The authors propose a model divided into three stages meant to help an analyst identify the fundamental

---

[58] Steven R. Mann, "Chaos Theory and Strategic Thought," *Parameters* 22, no. 3 (Autumn 1992): 67.

[59] For example, David A. Schum, *Evidence and Inference for the Intelligence Analyst,* Volumes I and II (Lanham, MD: University Press of America, 1987); Defense Intelligence Agency (DIA), *Methodology Catalog: an Aid to Intelligence Analysts and Forecasters* (Washington, DC: DIA, 1983) and Jerome K. Clauser and Sandra Weir, *Intelligence Research Methodology* (State College, PA: HRB-Singer, Inc., 1975).

potential for strife, the movement of possible strife into probable strife, and whether probable strife will turn into real conflict.[60] Many technology companies produce software to assist the user in problem solving by guiding him through a structured methodology and product demonstrations via the Internet.[61]

Exploitation of Structured Methodologies

A structured methodology provides a demonstrable means to reach a conclusion. Even if it can be proven that, in a given circumstance, both intuitive and scientific approaches provide the same degree of accuracy, structured methods have significant and unique value in that they can be easily taught to other analysts as a way to structure and balance their analysis. It is difficult, if not impossible, to teach an intelligence analyst how to conduct accurate intuitive analysis. Intuition comes with experience. What is clear is that, even though a mixture of science and intuition is probably needed to produce superior qualitative intelligence analysis, structured methodologies are severely neglected. Even in the rare cases where a specific methodology is regularly used, there is too much reliance on only one method and not a mix of various methods. No one method is appropriate to every problem. What is needed is a set of analytical tools that can be applied individually or in combination as appropriate.

Why Are Structured Methodologies Not Used?

Structured thinking is radically at variance with the way in which the human mind is in the habit of working.[62] Most people are used to solving problems intuitively by trial and error. Breaking this habit and establishing a new habit of thinking is an extremely difficult task and probably the primary reason why attempts to reform intelligence analysis have failed in the past, and why intelligence budgets for analytical methodology have remained extremely small when compared to other intelligence functions.[63]

Under the accelerating pressures of time, intelligence analysts feel that structured analytical approaches are too cumbersome.[64] They also sense that with the increased use of structured methods comes increased accountability. An excessively burdened intelligence analyst is less confident in his own ability and will not unnecessarily expose himself to criticism. Reliance on intuition and the resistance to incorporate scientific approaches complicate the task of getting analysts to exploit structured methodologies to assist qualitative intelligence analysis.

---

[60] Ashley J. Tellis, Thomas S. Szayna, and James A. Winnefeld, *Anticipating Ethnic Conflict* (Santa Monica: The Rand Corporation 1997), 9.

[61] Marek J. Druzdzel, "Decision Analysis Software," 5 September 1998, *Decisions Systems Laboratory*, URL: <*http://www.lis.pitt.edu/~dsl/da-software.html*>, accessed 17 February 1999.

[62] Jones, *The Thinker's Toolkit*, 8.

[63] Andriole, "Indications, Warning, & Bureaucracies," 10-11.

[64] Eales, 121-124.

Intelligence analysts are also not exploiting structured methodologies when they conduct qualitative intelligence analysis because they are not convinced that this will improve their analysis. If empirical evidence shows that such an improvement will take place, then analysts may consider it worth the investment of time, effort, and risk required on their part to regularly exploit structured methodologies. However, if such empirical evidence shows that exploiting structured methodologies will not significantly improve qualitative intelligence analysis, then analysts can devote their time and effort to enhancing their intuitive skills.

The results from the series of experiments conducted for this study may provide some empirical data needed by intelligence analysts to make a decision on whether they should begin exploiting structured methodologies.

THE EXPERIMENT

The Control Group Versus the Experimental Group

Arguments both for and against the use of structured methodologies to improve qualitative intelligence analysis may have merit. Therefore, empirical evidence is needed to determine if exploiting structured methodologies will improve qualitative intelligence analysis. A direct comparison of analytical results derived from using a structured method with results derived solely from an intuitive approach is necessary for a relevant experiment. The author designed an experiment to make such a comparison.

The purpose of the experiment was to compare the analytical conclusions drawn by individual analysts in two different groups: a control group and an experimental group. Individual analysts in the control group would use the traditional intuitive approach to analyze two different qualitative intelligence problems. Analysts in the experimental group would exploit a specific structured methodology to aid them in their analysis of these same two problems. Analysts' answers would be scored as either correct or incorrect and compared statistically to determine whether the experimental group did significantly better than the control group.

Competing Hypotheses and Level of Significance

The experiment would test the truth of both the null hypothesis (H_0) and the alternative, or research, hypothesis (H_1). The level of significance was set at .05 before the experiment was conducted.[65]

---

[65] A one-tailed test of statistical significance is appropriate to determine whether to reject the null and research hypotheses, given their directional nature. Two-tailed tests are appropriate to determine if factors such as rank, experience, education or branch of service may have affected the results of the experiment, as no assumption was made as to how these factors may influence qualitative intelligence analysis. The author is grateful to Francis J. Hughes, JMIC Faculty, for invaluable assistance in identifying statistical methods appropriate to this study.

H_0: Exploiting structured methodologies *will not* improve qualitative intelligence analysis.

H_1: Exploiting structured methodologies *will* improve qualitative intelligence analysis.

Determining Sample Size and Choosing a Statistical Test

Due to the real-world commitments of the intelligence analysts at each JIC, it was impossible to predetermine how many analysts would be sampled during the experiment. Not knowing the sample size or expected frequencies of each cell beforehand made it impossible to select an appropriate statistical test to analyze the information until all of it was collected. On the day of the experiment each JIC Commander decided which intelligence analysts would be available to participate. The decision of who would participate was made based upon that day's schedule as driven by operational requirements. The decision was not made based upon an attempt to alter the results of the experiment.

The available analysts from each JIC were randomly assigned to either the control or experimental group. Both the control group and the experimental group had 13 analysts each. The total number of analysts sampled (N) during the experiment was 26. Due to the small sample size and associated low cell frequencies, Fisher's Exact Probability Test was used to determine statistical significance for the hypotheses and for the influence of the controlled factors (rank, experience, education and branch of service).[66]

Collection Procedures

Analysts in both control and experimental groups completed a one-page questionnaire to provide the demographic information needed to crosscheck the validity of the results gathered from the experiment. Each analyst was asked to identify any training or familiarity they had with using various structured analytical methodologies and how frequently, if ever, they used structured methodologies during real-world analysis. Then the analysts in the control group were dismissed and asked to return at a later time. The analysts in the experimental group were given an hour of training on a specific structured methodology—hypothesis testing. The training was standardized at each JIC and taught from the same lesson plan and workbook.[67] The analysts in the experimental group were asked not to discuss their training with the analysts in the control group until after the experiment.

When the analysts assigned to the control group returned, the two groups were segregated. Each analyst in each group was then given a map, both intelligence scenarios,

---

[66] Marija J. Norusis, *SPSS 8.0 Guide to Data Analysis* (Upper Saddle River, NJ: Prentice-Hall, 1998), 315. Fisher's Test produces a probability for a one-tailed test. Several theories address how one can use Fisher's Test to produce a probability for a two-tailed test. The most common method is to simply double the one-tailed test result, and not to exceed a probability of 1. Doubling the probability for one-tailed results is the method the author used. Other methods use more complicated mathematical formulas, but yield similar probabilities.

[67] Morgan D. Jones authored the Hypothesis Testing Lesson Plan and workbook, which were used by permission. For further information on his hypothesis testing methods, see Chapter 11 of Jones' *The Thinker's Toolkit.*

and an answer sheet for each scenario. (See information on following pages). Each person was asked to analyze the first scenario, then to complete the answer sheet as individuals within one hour. Once this task was completed, they were asked to analyze the second scenario and complete its answer sheet as individuals within 30 minutes. At the end of the allotted time they were asked to turn in their completed answer sheets and any other notes they had made. Both groups were given the same amount of time to analyze the scenarios and to complete the answer sheets, so neither group had an advantage of time over the other. All notes made by the analysts were collected to determine what approach analysts in the control group used and to ensure that analysts in the experimental group properly applied the hypothesis testing method. All analysts were interviewed after completing the experiment to gain further insights into how they approached analyzing intelligence problems presented both in the experiment and in their official duties.

Only the first question on the answer sheet for each intelligence problem was scored. It was scored as either correct or incorrect. For the first intelligence scenario the correct answer was to expect an attack at Port Mia. For the second scenario the correct answer was that the intentions of the adversary government were peaceful.

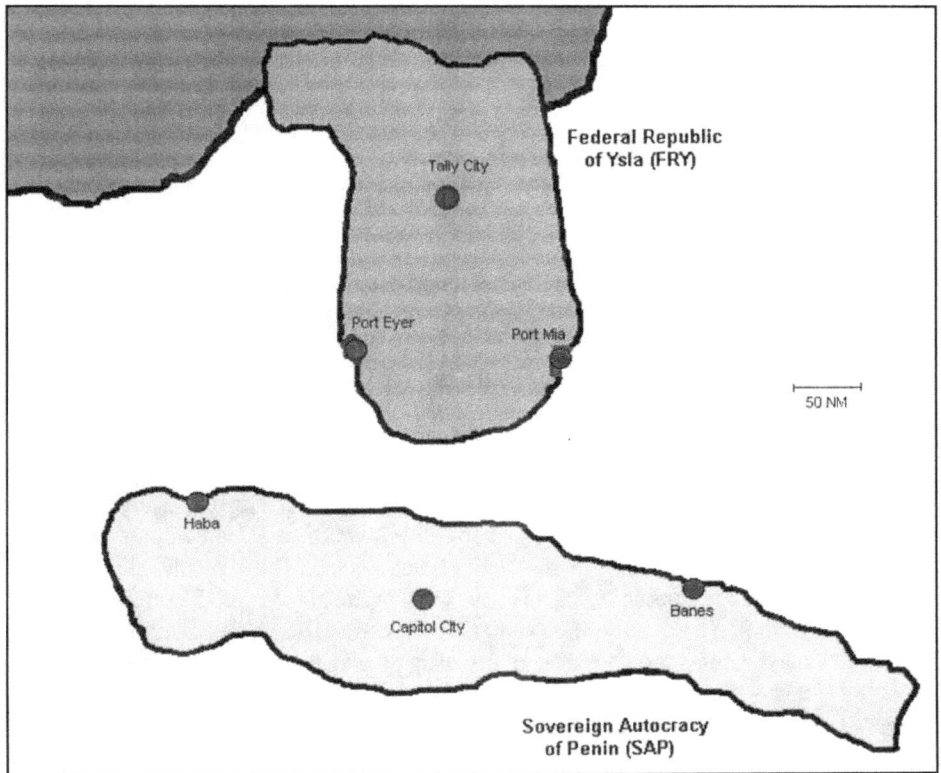

Map for Intelligence Scenarios 1 and 2.

INTELLIGENCE SCENARIO 1

You provide strategic intelligence to the military and political leaders of your country, the Federal Republic of Ysla (FRY). The Sovereign Autocracy of Penin (SAP) and FRY are at war. SAP is conducting air reconnaissance, special operations, and air bombing attacks against FRY to prepare the way for a military attack. You have determined that due to the unique geography of your country and the limited amphibious capabilities of the SAP military, only two places in FRY are vulnerable to an amphibious attack by the SAP military. SAP naval forces can conduct operations out to 250 nautical miles. To best defend FRY you need to determine how and where the SAP military invasion will occur. Using the above assumptions and the scenario map, conduct an analysis of the following intelligence information (it is listed chronologically). Keep in mind that the FRY National Leadership is concerned the SAP military will launch a diversionary attack against Port Mia while the main attack is against Port Eyer. They want your analysis to include information on whether the SAP military is planning to use deception, diversion, or neither in conjunction with their attack.

Based on order of battle from multiple sources you know the majority of SAP naval/ amphibious forces are docked in port at Banes. Multiple sources indicate that SAP has relocated most of its ground forces to Haba and reassigned them to the recently modernized Third SAP Corps. COMINT reporting indicates that a new SAP Marine General was assigned as Commander of the Third SAP Corps. On January 28th open sources report that General Sage, the SAP Supreme Military Commander, left SAP to encourage the nearby countries to remain neutral during the conflict; his travel schedule and return date are unknown. The SAP Government publicly announced a ban on all visits to the SAP coast. 007, one of FRY's top HUMINT agents working in Capitol City, reported the SAP main attack will occur near Port Eyer and may be preceded by diversionary attacks elsewhere in FRY. 086, another FRY spy, working near Banes reported that SAP would land a small force at Port Mia before the main attack at Port Eyer. Multiple sources indicate the SAP military has conducted amphibious exercises with submerged obstacles. COMINT reporting indicated major moves of SAP marine military forces to the northwest part of SAP. COMINT reports also indicated a major movement of forces from Capitol City to the northeast. SAP bombing raids against Port Eyer number twice that against Port Mia. The SAP bombing of Ports Eyer and Mia has restricted the flow of traffic in and out of both areas. The majority of SAP air reconnaissance and special operations have been against Port Eyer. On February 19th, FRY air reconnaissance showed no changes in ships at Haba. On February 25th, FRY air reconnaissance showed no change in shipping traffic in Banes. On March 8th, FRY air reconnaissance of both Haba and Banes showed increased shipping around Banes only. On March 30th, FRY air reconnaissance showed 20 new landing craft docked at Haba; air reconnaissance at Banes on the same day was inconclusive due to weather.

QUESTIONS FOR INTELLIGENCE SCENARIO 1

1. Where and how will the SAP's military attack FRY?

2. Support your conclusion. (Please attach any other notes you made.)

3. What other possible courses of action did you consider?

4. What analytical method did you use? How did you analyze this scenario?

5. Was this scenario similar to another current or historical event?

6. What is your assessment of the validity of this experiment?

7. Please provide your name and rank. Your answers and identity will be kept anonymous!

INTELLIGENCE SCENARIO 2

Due in part to your exceptional analysis, the Federal Republic of Ysla (FRY) successfully defended itself from a major invasion by the Sovereign Autocracy of Penin (SAP). On May 8th of last year, the war ended in a stalemate after the U.S. intervened, and both FRY and SAP governments signed an armistice. U.S. troops established a presence in FRY to deter SAP from attacking again. The SAP Government is concerned that the FRY military may launch an attack on SAP. The SAP Government wants the U.S. to withdraw its forces from FRY before SAP signs any peace treaty. Tensions between the FRY and SAP remained high throughout the year. However, at the beginning of the New Year, the leader of SAP, President Castrol, appeared to be making peaceful overtures to the FRY Government. Your superiors have asked you to analyze the evidence below and determine whether the SAP Government has new and peaceful intentions.

On January 15th, the SAP News Agency, the official news agency of the SAP Government, described an interview that President Castrol had with the editorial committee of a Caribbean newspaper, *The Island Times* on January 10th. President Castrol proposed: "a peace agree-ment...may be concluded between SAP and FRY and the military forces of both countries may be cut drastically under the condition where the U.S. imperialist troops are withdrawn from FRY."

In a subsequent meeting with U.S. Senator Harley (Democrat) in mid-January, President Castrol made it clear that a peace agreement between SAP and FRY could be concluded before U.S. forces were withdrawn.

U.S. intercepts since mid-February of secure, high-level, SAP military command communications have revealed no indications of unusual military activities or preparations for hostilities.

Over the next seven months the SAP News Agency was consistent in reporting the new peace proposals, only occasionally reverting to a "hard line" stance and then attributing this stance to unnamed spokesmen.

Last year, shortly after the armistice was signed, Red Cross delegates from both FRY and SAP began meeting on a regular basis to share information to help locate and identify soldiers from both sides who were missing in action during the war. Initially, the SAP News Agency coverage of the Red Cross meetings was very negative. After January of this year, however, the tone of the coverage changed. The reporting became essentially factual and objective.

In February of this year, the SAP Government began a national blood donation campaign claiming shortages, although the reason for shortages was not disclosed nor had there been any major disaster causing shortages to occur. Later the same month, President Castrol gave another "unofficial" interview to a journalist from the *Washington Times*. In the interview President Castrol again iterated that a peace treaty could be signed between SAP and FRY before U.S. troops withdraw from FRY.

INTELLIGENCE SCENARIO 2

On March 15th, SAP announced the execution of five SAP nationals who were members of a FRY spy ring during the war.

The commander-in-chief of SAP armed forces retired on March 29th and was replaced by the deputy commander-in-chief.

The number and tone of SAP propaganda broadcasts changed noticeably in the spring. The number of anti-FRY radio broadcasts declined from about 25 per day to about 16 broadcasts per day. Also, the usual abusive and slanderous words used in the broadcasts were toned down considerably.

In April, the two governments signed an agreement allowing each other's military attaches unrestricted movement without pre-travel approval.

Monitoring of SAP News Agency wire service releases containing anti-FRY statements declined from a high of 27 percent in January to 10 percent in April.

Over the past six months SAP military training has maintained its normal cycle.

Training flights of SAP fighter aircraft and bombers have been significantly curtailed over the past four months. In that same period the FRY Government has not detected any attempt by the SAP Government to infiltrate agents or armed guerrillas

The unusually large number of SAP reservists called to active duty during the war will be discharged this month.

SAP ground-force medical units conducted a large-scale, out-of-training-cycle exercise yesterday.

U.S. photoreconnaissance reveals that dozens of landing craft used in the SAP military operations against FRY during the war have not been repaired.

QUESTIONS FOR INTELLIGENCE SCENARIO 2

1. What are the intentions of the SAP Government?

2. Support your conclusion. (Please attach any other notes you made.)

3. List all the possibilities you considered.

4. What analytical method did you use? How did you analyze this scenario?

5. Was this scenario similar to another current/historical event?

6. What is your assessment of the validity of this experiment?

7. Please provide your name and rank. Your answers and identity will be kept anonymous!

HYPOTHESIS TESTING ILLUSTRATION: INTELLIGENCE SCENARIO 1

Possible Hypotheses are:

H1: Main attack at Port Eyer, no major deception or diversion.

H2: Main attack at Port Eyer, with deception pointing to Port Mia.

H3: Main attack at Port Eyer, with diversionary attack at Port Mia.

H4: Main attack at Port Mia, no major deception or diversion.

H5: Main attack at Port Mia, with deception pointing to Port Eyer.

H6: Main attack at Port Mia, with diversionary attack at Port Eyer.

EVIDENCE	H_1	H_2	H_3	H_4	H_5	H_6
1. Multiple Sources (MS), majority of SAP Naval forces at Banes.	I	C	C	C	I	I
2. MS, majority of ground forces assigned to modernized Third Corps at Haba	C	I	C	I	C	C
3. COMINT, new Marine general commanding Third SAP Corps	C	I	I	I	C	C
4. 28 Jan, General Sage visits neutral countries; return date unknown	?	?	?	?	?	?
5. SAP bans visits to coasts	C	C	C	C	C	C
6. 007, main attack at Port Eyer with possible diversion	I	I	C	I	C	I
7. 086, small force attacks Port Mia then main attack at Port Eyer	I	I	C	I	C	I
8. SAP conducts amphibious exercises with submerged obstacles	C	C	C	C	C	C
9. COMINT, Marines move to northwest SAP	C	I	I	I	C	C
10. COMINT, major movement of forces from Capitol City to northeast SAP	I	C	C	C	I	I
11. SAP bombs Port Eyer 2X as much as Port Mia	C	I	C	I	C	C
12. SAP bombing restricts traffic in/out of both ports	C	C	C	C	C	C
13. Majority of SAP air recon and SOF directed against Port Eyer	C	I	C	I	C	C
14. 19 Feb and 25 Feb, no change in ships at Haba or shipping at Banes	I	C	I	C	C	C
15. 8 Mar, increase in shipping at Banes	I	C	I	C	C	C
16. 30 Mar, 20 new landing craft at Haba; Recon at Banes is inconclusive due to weather	C	I	C	?	?	?

Hypothesis Testing Matrix Example for Intelligence Scenario 1.

Note: Letters characterize the attributed relationship between evidence and hypothesis: consistent=C; inconsistent=I; ambiguous=?; evidence that is either consistent or ambiguous for all hypotheses is "lined out" to show that it was considered, then disregarded, in favor of more telling "directional" evidence.

HYPOTHESIS TESTING ILLUSTRATION: INTELLIGENCE SCENARIO 2

Possible Hypotheses are:

H_1: Peace
H_2: Business-as-Usual
H_3: Deception.

EVIDENCE	H_1	H_2	H_3
1. Jan-Apr, SAP News Agency Anti-FRY statements decline to 10%	C	I	C
2. Jan-Apr, SAP fighter/bomber training sorties decline	C	I	C
3. Jan-Apr, FRY detects no SAP infiltration attempts	C	I	I
4. Jan-Jun, SAP military training cycle is normal	~~C~~	~~C~~	~~C~~
5. Jan 15, Castrol proposes peace with FRY	C	I	C
6. Mid-Jan, Castrol says peace before U.S. troops leave	C	I	C
7. Feb, SAP News Agency begins positive reporting of ICRC	C	I	C
8. Early Feb, SAP Government blood drive	I	C	C
9. Mid-Feb, no unusual SAP C2 activity	~~C~~	~~C~~	~~C~~
10. Late-Feb, Castrol says peace treaty before U.S. leaves	C	I	C
11. Feb-Aug, SAP News Agency consistently reports peace proposal	C	I	C
12. Mar 15, SAP executes members of FRY spy-ring	I	C	I
13. Mar 29, SAP CINC retires and replaced by his Deputy	~~C~~	~~C~~	~~C~~
14. April, FRY and SAP sign agreement allowing unrestricted travel	C	I	I
15. April, SAP discharges reservists called up during the war	C	I	I
16. April, SAP conducts a large, out-of-cycle medical exercise	I	C	C
17. April, SAP landing craft remain unrepaired	C	I	I
18. Spring, SAP propaganda broadcasts decrease in number and tone	C	I	I

Hypothesis Testing Matrix Example for Intelligence Scenario 2[68]

---

[68] Although assigning a C, I, or ? to an individual line of evidence is a subjective judgment, by visually displaying the evidence and hypotheses in a matrix the analyst can better judge each piece of evidence then aggregate all the evidence to determine which hypothesis is most likely true. Subjective judgments and intuition still play an inescapable role in analysis. Individual analysts will seldom assign C, I, or ? in the same way, but by visually displaying it, other analysts can question their logic, readily identify which pieces of evidence they disagree on, and more quickly form a consensus.

Experimental Results Arrayed in Contingency Tables

Tables 1 and 2 summarize the responses given by analysts in the control and the experimental groups to each intelligence scenario. Tables 3-10 show how the analysts answered each intelligence scenario based on rank, years of experience, level of education, and branch of service.

A. Comparison of Responses between Control and Experimental Groups:

	Control Group	Experimental Group
# of Incorrect Answers	11	10
# of Correct Answers	2	3

Table 1. Response by Group to Intelligence Scenario 1

	Control Group	Experimental Group
# of Incorrect Answers	4	0
# of Correct Answers	9	13

Table 2. Response by Group to Intelligence Scenario 2

B. Comparison of Responses between Civilian/Officer and Enlisted:

	Civilian/Officer	Enlisted
# of Incorrect Answers	9	12
# of Correct Answers	3	2

Table 3. Response by Rank to Intelligence Scenario 1

	Civilian/Officer	Enlisted
# of Incorrect Answers	1	3
# of Correct Answers	11	11

Table 4. Response by Rank to Intelligence Scenario 2

C. Comparison of Responses Based on Years of Experience:

	Less than 10 years	10 years or more
# of Incorrect Answers	12	9
# of Correct Answers	2	3

Table 5. Response by Years of Experience to Intelligence Scenario 1

C. Comparison of Responses Based on Years of Experience: (Cont'd)

	Less than 10 years	10 years or more
# of Incorrect Answers	2	2
# of Correct Answers	12	10

Table 6. Response by Years of Experience to Intelligence Scenario 2

D. Comparison of Responses Based on Level of Education:

	<Bachelor Degree	Bachelor Degree or Higher
# of Incorrect Answers	12	9
# of Correct Answers	2	3

Table 7. Response by Level of Education to Intelligence Scenario 1

	<Bachelor Degree	Bachelor Degree or Higher
# of Incorrect Answers	2	2
# of Correct Answers	12	10

Table 8. Response by Level of Education to Intelligence Scenario 2

E. Comparison of Responses between Military Services:

	Navy/Marine	Army/Air Force
# of Incorrect Answers	9	12
# of Correct Answers	1	4

Table 9. Response by Branch of Service to Intelligence Scenario 1

	Navy/Marine	Army/Air Force
# of Incorrect Answers	0	4
# of Correct Answers	10	12

Table 10. Response by Branch of Service to Intelligence Scenario 2

Analytical Strategy

Fisher's Exact Probability Test was used to statistically analyze the data and determine whether the null hypothesis could be rejected. This formula was also used in a two-tailed test to measure any variances in responses based on the different demographic groups. In these cases Fisher's Test would measure the probability that the differences in the answers were caused by some other factor than the use of a structured methodology to assist in qualitative intelligence analysis. The original tables displaying demographic data for the control and experimental groups contained several columns, not just two. However, Fisher's Test can be used to measure data only in a two-by-two matrix, so it was necessary to modify the original tables by combining some columns to arrange the data in an appropriate two-by-two matrix.

CONSIDERATIONS AND LIMITATIONS

Although this experiment did collect and analyze data on several different factors that might affect the answers an analyst would provide, it could not identify and analyze all factors. To encourage individual participation an agreement was made that the results of individual analysts would not be released. To encourage the JICs to provide as many analysts as possible it was agreed that the specific results of each JIC would be made available only to that particular JIC. This experiment was designed to compare the answers given by the control and experimental groups; it would not compare JIC against JIC. Therefore, the way in which analysts were made available, driven as it was by real-world events, did not alter the validity of the experiment.

Designing the Experiment

Certainly, one can find some fault in both intelligence scenarios used during the experiment. Nevertheless, both scenarios were submitted to a rigorous pre-testing and revision process to ensure both scenarios were valid and reliable measures of an intelligence analyst's qualitative analytical capability during the time allotted for the experiment and appropriate for the structured methodology taught to the experimental group.

Several obstacles hinder the design of an intelligence scenario to measure the accuracy of an analyst's conclusions. A hypothetical scenario begs the question of whether one can authoritatively claim that a correct answer exists. Since the event never occurred, the burden is on the creator of the scenario to ensure only one conclusion can be drawn. In contrast, using an actual historical event as the basis for an intelligence scenario runs the risk that the analyst will recognize the scenario for what it is and base his conclusions on the known outcome rather than on the evidence presented. The intelligence scenarios used in the experiment were based on actual historical events.

The first scenario was developed in coordination with Tom Murray, former CIA analyst and trainer and currently Senior Vice President of Sequoia Associates, Incorporated. The scenario was based on known strategic intelligence possessed by

German intelligence prior to the invasion of Normandy during World War II. It was necessary to alter some of the evidence such as the names of individuals, units, and geographic locations in the scenario to disguise the fact that this scenario was based on the invasion at Normandy, but the basic evidence remained unchanged. In this scenario the analysts were asked to determine where the actual invasion would occur.

The second intelligence scenario was based upon a case study presented in *Intelligence Research and Methodology,* by Jerome Clauser and Sandra Weir. The case study examined a series of incidents in which it appeared the North Korean Government was making a sincere effort to improve peace on the peninsula in the 1970's.[69] This scenario was modified with the assistance of Morgan D. Jones. The subjects were asked to determine whether the adversary in the scenario was sincerely pursuing peace, using peace as a deception, or conducting business as usual.

Various students at the JMIC tested both intelligence scenarios before they were used in the experiment at the JICs. The students were asked to analyze both scenarios and complete an answer sheet. The answer sheet asked them to draw some conclusions and also asked whether they recognized the scenarios as any actual historical event. The scenarios were then modified and given to another group of students to test. In the final round of testing only three out of 20 students recognized that the first scenario was related to the Normandy invasion; however, only one of the three who recognized the historical link provided the correct answer. None of the students could identify the actual event used as a basis for the second scenario. During the actual experiment at the JICs, five of the 26 subjects identified the Normandy invasion as the basis for the first intelligence scenario. Four of these five were in the control group and the other was in the experimental group. Of the five only one in the experimental group and another in the control group provided the correct answer to the first scenario. No one at the JICs identified the actual historical event used as a basis for the second scenario. These checks on the historical identifiability of the scenarios address the potential concern of "analysis as art" proponents that deep familiarity with a particular region or problem would affect the outcome of this or a similar experiment. It would appear that this concern, though well-founded, can be overcome by careful selection of scenarios. Scenario construction or borrowing is not a simple matter, as a real-world "outcome" must be captured to ensure a "correct" answer is known.

The questions on the answer sheets were open-ended rather than multiple choice. Although using a multiple choice test simplifies the scoring process, it does not accurately portray how analysts provide answers outside the classroom. A multiple choice test defines the range of options available; in qualitative intelligence analysis, defining and narrowing the range of options is a part of the answer in itself. Asking open-ended questions provided insights into how many possible hypotheses each analyst considered and how specific a response each analyst felt confident in providing.

---

[69] Clauser and Weir, 358-369.

Time Spent Analyzing the Scenarios

Rather than allow the analysts to work at their own pace, a specific period of time was allotted to work each problem; however, the analysts were allowed to turn in their answer sheets anytime before the allotted time expired. Although it would be interesting to compare the number of correct answers with the amount of time spent on the problem, it would be of little help in determining whether exploiting structured methodologies will improve qualitative intelligence analysis. Based on observations made during the experiment, it seems that the amount of time spent on analyzing a problem had little to do with the analyst correctly answering a problem or using a structured method. Both control and experimental groups had analysts who completed both problems quickly and had analysts who used the entire amount of time allotted.

Most analysts work under a deadline. Allotting a fixed amount of time to solve each problem put pressure on the analyst (simulating real-world constraints) and ensured the answer sheets were returned in time to be included in this study. It also held the variable of time constant so the results of the experiment were less likely to be tainted by the time factor. Many of the analysts remarked that they enjoyed the opportunity to concentrate on a specific problem without being interrupted.

THE FINDINGS

This exploratory research provides empirical evidence suggesting that exploitation of a structured methodology (hypothesis testing in this example) will improve qualitative intelligence analysis. Even though this evidence is for a narrowly defined instance (the second intelligence scenario) and not conclusive, such evidence did not exist before this experiment was conducted. Factors such as rank, experience, education, and branch of service did not appear to affect the results.

Description of the Findings

As Tables 1 and 2 show, the overall qualitative intelligence analysis of those in the experimental group was better than that of those in the control group for both scenarios. Despite this, the improvement measured in the first scenario did not meet the threshold of statistical significance (see results for Table 1 in Table 11). Nor did the probabilities computed for Tables 3-10 meet the established threshold of statistical significance (see results for Tables 3-10 in Table 11), confirming that the differences in responses are probably not due to these factors. However, the improved qualitative analysis of the experimental group over that of the control group in the second scenario was statistically significant (see results for Table 2 in Table 11).

Table No.	Description	Scenario No.	Fisher's Probability
1	Control and Experiment	1	.5
2	Control and Experiment	2	.048
3	Rank	1	.844
4	Rank	2	.718
5	Experience	1	.844
6	Experience	2	1.0
7	Education	1	.844
8	Education	2	1.0
9	Branch of Service	1	.686
10	Branch of Service	2	.244

Table 11. Probabilities that Results are Due to Chance

Expectations

The results were surprising. The author expected a significant improvement in qualitative intelligence analysis in the first scenario, whose inherent complexity, it seemed, would give the analysts who used the hypothesis testing method an advantage over those who did not employ a structured method. But this advantage did not materialize. Most of the analysts using hypothesis testing seemed to have had difficulty identifying all of the possible hypotheses and determining the consistency of each piece of evidence with each hypothesis.

Because the second scenario was simple and straightforward, the author thought that there would be little or no advantage to be gained by structuring the problem and sorting the evidence. In the event, however, the structured approach proved more effective.

In hindsight it was asking too much to expect the analysts to proficiently apply the hypothesis testing method to complex problems like the first intelligence scenario after just one hour of training. This may explain, in part, why the experimental group did not perform significantly better than the control group on the first scenario. Because the first scenario, with six hypotheses to consider, is more complicated than the second scenario, with only three hypotheses, one may be tempted to conclude that the hypothesis testing method is useful for structuring only simple problems. Nevertheless, based on the information gathered during this experiment, the author would guess that the hypothesis testing method can be useful in structuring more intricate problems, provided that the analyst has been adequately trained to proficiently apply the method.

What Does All This Mean?

Quite simply, the experimental group performed significantly better on the second intelligence scenario than did the control group. The improvement appears to be due to members of the experimental group using a particular structured methodology while the members of the control group did not use any structured methodology to aid their analysis. The improvement does not appear to be a consequence of rank, experience, education, or branch of service. The improvement measured in qualitative intelligence analysis during the first intelligence scenario is not significant.

Why Improvement in the Second Scenario But Not the First?

The first scenario may have affected the control group's analysis of the second scenario. In the first scenario it was obvious that some form of deception was being used; the problem was determining which attack was real and which was the deception. The second scenario was more clear and direct; however, some analysts may have been biased and assumed deception was being used in the second scenario because of their recent exposure to the use of deception in the first scenario. It appears that those analysts who used the hypothesis testing method were better able to remain objective and analyze the evidence in the second scenario without being influenced by the first scenario. It seems the analysts who based their analysis solely on their intuition were less objective in their analysis.

Another Approach to Analyzing the Data

During the experiment each analyst was asked one question from both intelligence scenarios. Their answers were marked as either correct or incorrect. Thus, an analyst who answered both questions correctly scored 100 percent. If an analyst answered one question correctly and the other incorrectly, he scored 50 percent. If he answered both questions incorrectly, he scored 0 percent. The scores from analysts who used a structured methodology ranged from 50-100 percent. The analysts who did not use a structured methodology ranged in scores from 0-50 percent. While three analysts in the experimental group answered both questions correctly, no one in the control group answered both questions correctly. By this measure, exploiting a structured methodology improved qualitative intelligence analysis.

To Reject H_0 or Not?

Considering all the arguments, the information collected, and the analysis and interpretation of that information, the null hypothesis—that exploiting structured methodologies *will not* improve qualitative intelligence analysis—can be rejected. Of course there are several qualifiers that affect the veracity of the alternate hypothesis— that exploiting structured methodologies *will* improve qualitative intelligence analysis. The single most critical qualifier is that analysts must be adequately trained to ensure they are able to proficiently apply the appropriate structured methodology.

Unquestionably one can create a problem where the answer is so obvious that a structured methodology will be of no benefit. Likewise, one can design a scenario so complicated and ambiguous that the correct answer will never be revealed. Nevertheless, as this experiment demonstrated, there are instances where qualitative intelligence analysis can be improved by exploiting structured methodologies. Only by applying different structured methodologies to different types of intelligence problems will one find out where and when structured methods are most effective.

This experiment examined only one structured methodology—hypothesis testing. Other experiments that examine different methods, different problems, and utilize different analysts from different agencies could be pursued by other investigators. In the meantime, analysts within the Intelligence Community should be encouraged to exploit various structured methodologies.

IMPLICATIONS AND RECOMMENDATIONS

A Conclusion

This study has produced an answer to the question: "Will exploiting structured methodologies improve qualitative intelligence analysis?" The approach taken to answer the question was straightforward. Competing hypotheses were developed based on the research question, arguments supporting both hypotheses were explored, an impartial experiment was designed to provide empirical evidence, and a statistical test was used to determine the significance of the evidence produced. For both scenarios the analysts who used structured methods outperformed the analysts who did not. The improvement measured in the second intelligence scenario was statistically significant; therefore, the null hypothesis—that exploiting structured methodologies *will not* improve qualitative intelligence analysis—was rejected.

The author has determined that exploiting structured methodologies will improve qualitative intelligence analysis. There are, however, several qualifiers. The improvement is not necessarily automatic or significant for every case. Intelligence analysts must be adequately trained to select an appropriate structured methodology or combination of methodologies germane to the problem and apply the method(s) proficiently. A more precise conclusion drawn from the experiment as presented in this study is: "Exploiting structured methodologies *can* improve qualitative intelligence analysis." Further research is needed to definitively answer the original research question.

Other Insights

Based on the numerous interviews the author conducted with intelligence analysts from many different intelligence units and agencies, it is apparent that more basic research is needed in this area of intelligence analysis. Nearly every analyst had a different definition of intelligence analysis. Most analysts believe that analysis occurs automatically as they gather information and prepare that information for dissemination. It is not a function for which they specifically allocate time.

Analysis involves critical thinking. Structured methodologies do not perform the analysis for the analyst; the analyst still must do his own thinking. But by structuring a problem the analyst is better able to identify relevant factors and assumptions, formulate and consider different outcomes, weigh different pieces of evidence, and make decisions based on the available information. While exploiting a structured methodology cannot guarantee a correct answer, using a structured methodology ensures that analysis is performed and not overlooked.

From the discussions with the test subjects after the experiment it became obvious to the author that analysts in the control group were not as clear in their thinking as the analysts in the experimental group. After reading the scenarios members of the control group formed a conclusion, then went back to the scenario to find evidence that supported their conclusion and ignored contradictory evidence. When asked to justify their answers, analysts in the control group often cited some "key" information that gave them a flash of insight. Members of the control group seemed to be looking for the one piece of information—the "Holy Grail"— that would make sense of everything else. This approach flies in the face of the fact that, more often than not, qualitative intelligence analysis must be accomplished with incomplete information.

Members of the experimental group examined all evidence provided in the scenario prior to making their decision. They felt confident that they were making the best decision they could with the amount of information available. They acknowledged that their decision may not be the right one and added that if more evidence became available they would reevaluate their conclusion taking into account this new information.

Even though most analysts had not received training in or used structured methods previously, analysts who received training in hypothesis testing expressed the opinion that exploiting such a method would aid and improve their analysis.

Recommendations

The author recommends that various structured methodologies be taught to all intelligence analysts of every service and agency during both initial and subsequent training. Intelligence analysts should be encouraged to use structured methodologies when drafting analytical narratives. Analysts should be expected to utilize structured methodologies to visually present their analysis during intelligence briefings. Also, intelligence units conducting real-world qualitative intelligence analysis should be encouraged to experiment with different structured methodologies and compete with other similar units in regular analytical exercises. The results from exploiting various structured methodologies from both real-world situations and during exercises should be published and shared with other intelligence units, services, and agencies.

Further Research

The results of this experiment need to be confirmed. The author recommends that a series of similar experiments be conducted, either separately or in any combination, to test other factors that may affect the outcome of qualitative intelligence analysis.

Reverse Order of Scenarios. Future researchers may wish to conduct the same experiment as the original except reverse the order in which the intelligence scenarios are given to the analysts. Alternatively the researcher may develop his own scenarios but present them to different test subjects in a different order and track the results to see if the order in which the scenarios were presented affected the results of their analysis.

Intensive Training. Expand the amount of time spent training the experimental group from one hour to three or more hours and include more complex problems. Use the same scenarios as in the original experiment to test this author's theory that more training would have allowed the analysts to proficiently apply the hypothesis testing method to more complicated problems such as the first intelligence scenario.

Sophisticated Scenario. Future researchers may wish to conduct a similar experiment using a more sophisticated scenario to determine whether design flaws in the original scenarios affected the results of the original experiment.

Before and After. Instead of dividing analysts into control and experimental groups, have them analyze a scenario intuitively then train the same analysts in an appropriate structured methodology and have them analyze the same problem using the structured technique. Compare their first response with their second response and measure the improvement. A researcher utilizing this approach must develop a test to measure if the improvement arises from analysts' exploiting a structured method or simply from seeing the same or similar problem again.

Different Method. Conduct an experiment using a structured methodology other than hypothesis testing. The researcher must develop a new intelligence scenario appropriate to the structured methodology being tested.

Team Approach. Instead of measuring the responses of individuals, divide the analysts into teams and ask them to develop a consensus and answer the questions as a team. Have some teams use a structured methodology and have other teams use the traditional intuitive approach.

Measure Time. Instead of holding time as a constant, ask the analysts to solve the problems as quickly as possible and record how long it takes each analyst to solve the problem. Consider both accuracy and timeliness when measuring improvement in qualitative intelligence analysis.

Multiple Choice. Instead of asking open-ended questions, provide the analysts with a multiple choice answer sheet. This will simplify the scoring process and measure improvement while ensuring that every analyst considers the same possible outcomes.

Two-Tailed Test. Develop a hypothesis and design an experiment to measure if exploiting structured methodologies will cause a change in qualitative intelligence analysis in either direction. Also, other demographic information (such as gender, age, and personality type) should be collected and analyzed to see if these factors affect the results.

FINAL IMPRESSION

The author's motivation to conduct research into qualitative intelligence analysis comes from his own experience with the difficulties common to conducting and training others in analysis. Somewhat surprisingly, the present research has revealed how remarkably little analysts within the Intelligence Community appear to know about analytic methods, and less surprisingly, how great is the gap between their current and future analytic potential. It is clear to this researcher that a moderate investment in analytic training would substantially improve intelligence analysis.

BIBLIOGRAPHY

An analytic methodologist in Central Intelligence Agency's Directorate of Intelligence. Interview by author, 29 April 1999.

Andriole, Stephen J., Ph.D. *Handbook of Decision Support Systems.* Blue Ridge Summit, PA: Professional and Reference Books, 1989.

_____. *Handbook of Problem Solving: An Analytical Methodology.* New York: Petrocelli Books, Inc., 1983.

_____. "Indications, Warning, & Bureaucracies." *Military Intelligence Professional Bulletin* 10, no. 3 (July-September 1984): 6-12.

_____. *Methods for Intelligence Analysis, Production, and Presentation.* Unpublished research paper funded by DIA. Contract no. MDA908-83-C-1899. December 1983.

_____. Senior Intelligence Researcher and former Director of the Cybernetics Technology Office of the Advanced Research Projects Agency. Email interview by author, 15 December 1998.

"Art Hammer: The Numbers Man." *Economist,* 8 August 1998, 56.

Ball, W. Frank, Lieutenant Colonel, USMC (Retired), and Morgan D. Jones. "Improving Marine Commanders' Intuitive Decisionmaking Skills." *Marine Corps Gazette* (January 1996): 63-64.

Betts, Richard K., Ph.D. "Analysis, War, and Decision: Why Intelligence Failures Are Inevitable." *World Politics* 31, no. 1 (October 1978): 61-89.

_____. "Intelligence for Policymaking." *Washington Quarterly* 3, no. 3 (Summer 1980): 118-129.

_____. "Intelligence Warning: Old Problems, New Agendas." *Parameters* 28, no. 1 (Spring 1998): 26-35.

_____. "Policy-makers and Intelligence Analysts: Love, Hate, or Indifference?" *Intelligence and National Security* 3, no. 1 (January 1988): 184-189.

_____. "Strategic Intelligence Estimates: Let's Make Them Useful." *Parameters* 10, no.4 (Winter 1980): 20-27.

_____. "Surprise, Scholasticism, and Strategy: A Review of Ariel Levite's *Intelligence and Strategic Surprises* (New York: Columbia University Press, 1987)," *International Studies Quarterly* 33, no. 3 (September 1989): 329-343.

Brei, Captain William S. (USAF). *Getting Intelligence Right: The Power of Logical Procedure*. Occasional Paper Number Two. Washington, DC: Joint Military Intelligence College, 1996.

Brown, Thomas A., and Emir H. Shuford. *Quantifying Uncertainty Into Numerical Probabilities for The Reporting of Intelligence*. R-1185-ARPA. Santa Monica: The Rand Corporation, July 1973.

Clark, Robert M. *Intelligence Analysis: Estimation and Prediction*. Baltimore: American Literary Press, Inc., 1996.

Clauser, Jerome K., and Sandra Weir. *Intelligence Research Methodology*. State College, PA: HRB-Singer, Inc., 1975.

Coping with the Bounds: Speculations on Nonlinearity in Military Affairs. Ed. Tom Czerwinski. Washington, DC: National Defense University, 1998.

Critical Technologies for National Defense. Ed. J.S. Przemieniecki. Washington, DC: American Institute of Aeronautics and Astronautics, 1991.

Davis, Jack. "The Kent-Kendall Debate of 1949." *Studies in Intelligence* 35, no. 2 (Summer 1991): 37-49.

De Francesco, Henry F. *Quantitative Methods for Substantive Analysts*. Los Angeles: Melville Publishing Co., 1975.

Defense Intelligence Agency. *Methodology Catalog: An Aid to Intelligence Analysts and Forecasters*. DDE-2200-227-83. Washington, DC: DIA, December 1983.

DiPace, Tim. U.S. Atlantic Command Anti-Terrorism/Force Protection Officer. Interview by author, 19 March 1999.

"Don't Blame the CIA." *Economist*, 23 May 1998, 26.

Druzdzel, Marek J. "*Decision Analysis Software*." 5 September 1998. Decision Systems Laboratory. URL: <*http://www.lis.pitt.edu/~dsl/da-software.html*>. Accessed 17 February 1999.

Eales, Stewart Christopher. *Playing with Intelligence: Officer Application of Intelligence in the PURPLE SUNSET Wargame*. MSSI Thesis. Washington, DC: Joint Military Intelligence College, August 1997.

Finley, James P. "Intelligence Failure Matrix." *Military Intelligence Professional Bulletin* 20, no. 1 (January-March 1994): 14.

_____. "Nobody Likes to be Surprised: Intelligence Failures." *Military Intelligence Professional Bulletin* 20, no. 1 (January-March 1994): 15+.

Ford, Harold P. *Estimative Intelligence: The Purposes and Problems of National Intelligence Estimating.* New York: University Press of America, 1993.

Graves, David Lawrence, Captain, USAF. *Bayesian Analysis Methods for Threat Prediction.* MSSI Thesis. Washington, DC: Defense Intelligence College, 1993.

Grunwald, Michael, and others. "CIA Halted Plot to Bomb U.S. Embassy in Uganda." *Washington Post,* 25 September 1998, A27+.

Hall, Wayne M., Lieutenant Colonel, USA. "Intelligence Analysis in the 21st Century." *Military Intelligence Professional Bulletin* 18, no. 1 (January-March 1992): 6-12.

Hammond, James D. *So You Want to be an Intelligence Analyst?* Research Paper. Washington, DC: Defense Intelligence College, October 1983.

Hayes, Richard E. President of Evidence-Based Research, Inc. Interview by author, 9 February 1999.

Henry, Ryan, and C. Edward Peartree. "Military Theory and Information Warfare." *Parameters* 28, no. 3 (Autumn 1998): 121-135.

Hilsman, Roger. "Does the CIA Still Have a Role?" *Foreign Affairs* 74, no. 5 (September/October 1995): 104-116.

Hulnick, Arthur S. "Managing Intelligence Analysis: Strategies for Playing the End Game." *International Journal of Intelligence and Counterintelligence* 2, no. 3 (Fall 1988): 321-342.

"Hypothesis Testing: A Technique for Structuring Analysis." Outline, Lesson Plan, and Workbook. N.p., n.d. Provided on 15 March 1999 By Morgan D. Jones.

Inside CIA's Private World: Declassified Articles from the Agency's Internal Journal 1955-1992. Ed. H. Bradford Westerfield. New Haven: Yale University Press, 1995.

Jones, Morgan D. Former analyst for the Central Intelligence Agency and founder of Analytic Prowess, L.L.C. Interview by author, 15 March 1999.

_____. *The Thinker's Toolkit: 14 Powerful Techniques for Problem Solving.* New York: Random House, Inc., 1998.

Kahaner, Larry. *Competitive Intelligence: From Black Ops to Boardrooms — How Businesses Gather, Analyze, and Use Information to Succeed in the Global Marketplace.* New York: Simon & Schuster, 1996.

Kam, Ephraim. *Surprise Attack: The Victim's Perspective.* Cambridge, MA: Harvard University Press, 1988.

Keithly, David M. "Leading Intelligence in the 21st Century: Past as Prologue?" *Defense Intelligence Journal* 7, no. 1 (Spring 1998): 78-88.

Kent, Sherman. *Strategic Intelligence For American World Policy*. Princeton, NJ: Princeton University Press, 1949.

Kifner, John. "Raids by U.S. Agents and Tirana Police Reportedly Thwart Attack on Embassy." *New York Times*, 21 August 1998, A13.

Landers, Daniel F. "The Defense Warning System." *Defense Intelligence Journal* 3, no. 1 (Spring 1994): 21-32.

Loeb, Vernon and Walter Pincus. "New Spy Satellites at Risk Because Funding Is Uncertain, Pentagon Told." *Washington Post*, 12 November 1999, A7.

Manheim, Jarol B., and Richard C. Rich. *Empirical Political Analysis: Research Methods in Political Science*. New Jersey: Prentice-Hall, Inc., 1981.

Mann, Steven R. "Chaos Theory and Strategic Thought." *Parameters* 22, no. 3 (Autumn 1992): 54-68.

Manthorpe, William H.J. Jr. "From the Editor." *Defense Intelligence Journal* 7, no. 1 (Spring 1998): 3-5.

McCarthy, Mary. "The National Warning System: Striving for an Elusive Goal." *Defense Intelligence Journal* 3, no. 1 (Spring 1994): 5-19.

Murray, Thomas H., Ph.D. Former analyst and trainer for the Central Intelligence Agency and Senior Vice President of Sequoia Associates, Inc. Interview by author, 18 January 1999.

Neustadt, Richard, and Ernest May. *Thinking in Time*. New York: The Free Press, 1986.

New York Times, 7 June 1998 and 21 August 1998.

Newing, Rod. "Consumer Information is the Fuel of a New Industrial Revolution." *Financial Times*, 3 February 1999, B7.

Norusis, Marija J. *SPSS 8.0 Guide to Data Analysis*. Upper Saddle River, NJ: Prentice-Hall, 1998.

Nye, Joseph S. Jr. "Peering into the Future." *Foreign Affairs* 73, no. 4 (July/August 1994): 82-93.

Nye, Joseph S. Jr., and William A. Owens. "America's Information Edge." *Foreign Affairs* 75, no. 2 (March/April 1996): 20-25.

"An Orderly Approach to Intelligence Analysis." Instructor's manual. N.p., n.d. Provided on 18 January 1999 by the Senior Vice President of Sequoia Associates, Inc., Thomas H. Murray.

Owens, William A. "Intelligence in the 21st Century." *Defense Intelligence Journal* 7, no. 1 (Spring 1998): 25-45.

Peterson, John L. "Forecasting: It's Not Possible." *Defense Intelligence Journal* 3, no. 2 (Fall 1994): 37-45.

Pilzer, Paul Zane. *Unlimited Wealth*. New York: Crown Publishers, Inc., 1990.

Porteous, Samuel D. "Looking out for Economic Interests: An Increased Role for Intelligence." *Washington Quarterly* 19, no. 4 (Autumn 1996): 191-204.

Quantitative Approaches to Political Intelligence: The CIA Experience. Ed. Richards J. Heuer Jr. Boulder: Westview Press, Inc., 1978.

Resch, David T., Captain, USA. "Predictive Analysis: The Gap Between Academia and Practitioners." *Military Intelligence Professional Bulletin* 21, no. 2 (April-June 1995): 26-29.

Robbins, Carla Anne. "Intelligence Community is Criticized in Review." *Wall Street Journal*, 3 June 1998, A8.

Schweizer, Peter. "Growth in Economic Espionage." *Foreign Affairs* 75, no. 1 (January/February 1996): 9-14.

Schum, David A. *Evidence and Inference for the Intelligence Analyst*. Volumes I and II. Lanham, MD: University Press of America, 1987.

Shirley, Edward G. "CIA Needs Reform, Not New Missions." *Wall Street Journal*, 19 November 1998, A22.

Seib, Philip. "Intelligence Gathering Remains a Vital Function," 1 March 1999. *Dallas Morning News*. URL: <http://www.dia.ic.gov/admin/EARLYBIRD/990302/ s199990302/ gathering.htm>. Accessed 2 March 1999.

Siegel, Sydney. *Nonparametric Statistics For the Behavioral Sciences*. New York: McGraw-Hill Book Company, Inc., 1956.

Studeman, William O. "Leading Intelligence along the Byways of Our Future: Acquiring C4ISR Architectures for the 21st Century." *Defense Intelligence Journal* 7, no. 1 (Spring 1998): 47-65.

Tellis, Ashley J., Thomas S. Szayna, and James A. Winnefeld. *Anticipating Ethnic Conflict*. Santa Monica, CA: The Rand Corporation, 1997.

Tofœr, Alvin, and Heidi Tofœr. *War and Anti-War: Survival at the Dawn of the 21st Century*. New York: Little, Brown and Company, 1993.

Tufte, Edward R. *The Visual Display of Quantitative Information*. Cheshire, CT: Graphics Press, 1983.

Turner, Michael A. "Issues in Evaluating U.S. Intelligence." *International Journal of Intelligence and Counterintelligence* 5, no. 3 (Fall 1991): 275-284.

U.S. Commission on the Roles and Capabilities of the United States Intelligence Community. *Preparing for the 21st Century: An Appraisal of U.S. Intelligence.* Washington, DC: GPO, 1 March 1996. URL: *<http://www.access.gpo.gov/su_docs/dpos/epubs/int/int012.html>*.

Warning analyst at the National Warning Staff. Telephone interview by author, 5 November 1998.

Weiner, Tim, and James Risen. "Decision to Strike Factory in Sudan Based on Surmise: Inferred from Evidence." *New York Times*, 21 September 1998, A1.

Wohlstetter, Roberta. *Pearl Harbor: Warning and Decision.* Stanford, CA: Stanford University Press, 1962.

ABOUT THE AUTHOR

Master Sergeant Robert D. Folker, Jr. received the Master of Science of Strategic Intelligence degree from the Joint Military Intelligence College in 1999. He is currently Superintendent of the 325th Operations Support Squadron's Intelligence Flight at Tyndall Air Force Base, Florida. Since enlisting in the Air Force in 1986, MSgt Folker's assignments have included Non-Comissioned Officer in Charge (NCOIC), Special Intelligence Team at the Strategic Command's Intelligence and Warning Center, Offutt Air Force Base, Nebraska; NCOIC, Intelligence Element at the 80th Fighter Squadron, Kunsan Air Base, South Korea; and NCOIC, Mission Analysis Flight and Senior Analyst with the Contingency Airborne Reconnaissance Deployable Ground Station 2, Beale Air Force Base, California. MSgt Folker may be contacted at: *<robert.folker@tyndall.af.mil>*.

Joint Military Intelligence College

Occasional Papers

Unclassified papers are available through *<www.ntis.gov>*; selected papers are available through the U.S. Government Printing Office *<www.gpo.gov>*.

1. Classified paper.

2. *Getting Intelligence Right: The Power of Logical Procedure*, Capt (USAF) William S. Brei, 1996.

3. *An Office Manager's Guide to Intelligence Readiness*, Russell G. Swenson, 1996.

4. Classified paper.

5. *A Flourishing Craft: Teaching Intelligence Studies*, Papers Prepared for the 18 June 1999 JMIC Conference on Teaching Intelligence Studies at Colleges and Universities, 1999.

6. *Intelligence Essentials for Everyone*, Lisa Krizan, 1999.

7. *Intelligence Analysis in Theater Joint Intelligence Centers: An Experiment in Applying Structured Methods*, MSgt (USAF), Robert D. Folker, Jr., 2000.